ONE DAY
LEGACY
READ. WRITE. PRAY.

Song of Solomon

KIM ZIMMERMAN

Partnership
Publications

www.h2hp.com

Cover design by Brittney Hippensteel Graphic Design
Cover photos by Meagan Nicole Photography

One Day Legacy: Song of Solomon
by Kim Zimmerman

© 2016 by Kim Zimmerman

Published by
Partnership Publications
A Division of House Publications
11 Toll Gate Road, Lititz, PA, USA
Tele: 717.627.1996
www.h2hp.com

ISBN 13: 978-1539011323
ISBN 10: 1539011321

Printed in the United States of America

Contents

One day legacy

Read. Write. Pray.

I want to welcome you to One Day Legacy. Each day we are creating a legacy for ourselves and others. My prayer for you as you begin this legacy journey is to;

"Let the word of Christ dwell in you richly in all wisdom." (Colossians 3:16)

Jesus tells us in John 15 that His Words are to abide in us. I pray that as you journal, pray and read through this book of the Bible, that His Words abide, dwell and become life in you.

Document your spiritual journey as you learn about our Father God, His Son and The Holy Spirit.

Reading the Bible is like reading about a relationship in prayer with our Father. From start to finish, it is a continuous story; a dialogue from Him to us. We respond, then He responds. When we forget, He gives mercy. But where do we start in this relational dialogue? How do we enter?

Let's face it. We all struggle to find time to read the Bible or keep up with journaling. Sometimes we even lack the desire. So, in this journey, we will combine those two. Study of the Word and personal journal reflections will be brought together.

I write with a passion to empower you to read the Word, unleash a love of the Word and to begin a diet of devouring the Word. The Bible states that "Man shall not live by bread alone." That is an interesting concept, since fewer people are eating bread anyway because of gluten intolerance. But we are completely safe when we eat God's Word!

When we read the living Word of God, it changes us.

In this reading journal, we will read the Bible as we would read a prayer.

P - Prayer

R - Relationship

A - An attribute of God

Y - Yes. Yes, I will surrender. Yes, I will commit. Yes, I will.

Each day, read the selected chapter of the book and prayerfully answer the questions. I am certain that in every portion of scripture we can find each of the elements and apply them in our own lives. The questions encourage us to deeply consume the Word.

This is the process we will use in this devotional journal. Using the acronym PRAY we will read and journal our way through the Song of Solomon, soaking in His Word and learning of our Father God, His Son Jesus and the life-giving Holy Spirit.

Kim Zimmerman

Song of Solomon
introduction

The purpose of Song of Solomon, for this journal, is to enhance our love and passion for Jesus and to grow in our capacity to acknowledge the love our Father God has for us, and to return that love. I will use the term Song of Songs interchangeably with Song of Solomon, because I love the sound of Song of Songs – it creates a sense of worship just through the words.

Prayerfully read and find yourself in this progression and action that unfolds as we journey into the Song of Songs. By prayerfully reading, I suggest that you read the very words as a prayer. Give in to the pursuit of the Lover of our soul, to a place of wholeness and completeness in Him.

I am using the New King James Version in this book, as it is one of my favorite versions. You can use whichever version of the Bible you prefer. The Message is great, along with The Voice, New Living Translation (NLT), NASB or ESV.

Song of Solomon chapter 1

"Let him kiss me with the kisses of his mouth—
For your love is better than wine.
Because of the fragrance of your good ointments,
Your name is ointment poured forth;
Therefore the virgins love you.
Draw me away!"

Read and listen to the Word and write down the words or verses that inspire and encourage you.

P – Where do you see a prayer in this chapter?

_____

_____

_____

R – Where do you see the relationship between you and Jesus?
What verse do you see that in the most?

_____

_____

_____

Describe what prayer you see – feel – hear

_____

_____

_____

A – What attribute of God the Father do you see?
What attribute of Jesus do you see?

_____

_____

_____

Y – What is God asking you to say 'yes' to in this chapter?

_____

_____

_____

Journal

Write out a portion or all of chapter 1 as a prayer below, writing each verse back to God in prayer.

For example: God, kiss me with Your Word, so that Your Words fill my mouth.

Song of Solomon chapter 2

"My beloved spoke, and said to me:
"Rise up, my love, my fair one,
And come away...."

Read and listen to the Word and write down the words or verses
that inspire and encourage you.

P – Where do you see a prayer in this chapter?

_____

_____

_____

R – Where do you see the relationship between you and Jesus?
What verse do you see that in the most?

_____

_____

_____

Describe what prayer you see – feel – hear

_____

_____

_____

A – What attribute of God the Father do you see?
What attribute of Jesus do you see?

_____

_____

_____

Y – What is God asking you to say 'yes' to in this chapter?

_____

_____

_____

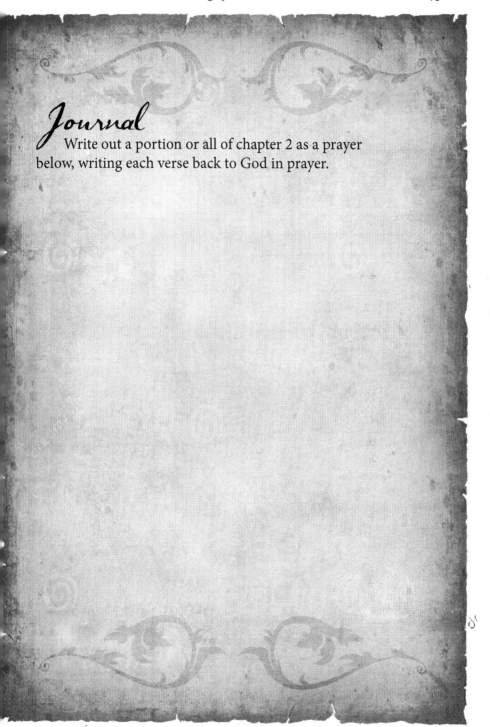

Journal

Write out a portion or all of chapter 2 as a prayer below, writing each verse back to God in prayer.

Song of Solomon chapter 3

"Scarcely had I passed by them,
When I found the one I love.
I held him and would not let him go…"

Read and listen to the Word and write down the words or verses that inspire and encourage you.

P – Where do you see a prayer in this chapter?

_____

_____

_____

R – Where do you see the relationship between you and Jesus? What verse do you see that in the most?

_____

_____

_____

Describe what prayer you see – feel – hear

_____

_____

_____

A – What attribute of God the Father do you see? What attribute of Jesus do you see?

_____

_____

_____

Y – What is God asking you to say 'yes' to in this chapter?

_____

_____

_____

Journal

Write out a portion or all of chapter 3 as a prayer below, writing each verse back to God in prayer.

Song of Solomon chapter 4

"Awake, O north wind,
And come, O south!
Blow upon my garden,
That its spices may flow out.
Let my beloved come to his garden
And eat its pleasant fruits."

Read and listen to the Word and write down the words or verses that inspire and encourage you.

P – Where do you see a prayer in this chapter?

_____

_____

_____

R – Where do you see the relationship between you and Jesus? What verse do you see that in the most?

_____

_____

_____

Describe what prayer you see – feel – hear

_____

_____

_____

A – What attribute of God the Father do you see? What attribute of Jesus do you see?

_____

_____

_____

Y – What is God asking you to say 'yes' to in this chapter?

_____

_____

_____

Journal

Write out a portion or all of chapter 4 as a prayer below, writing each verse back to God in prayer.

Song of Songs chapter 5

"I sleep, but my heart is awake;
It is the voice of my beloved!
He knocks, saying,
Open for me, my sister, my love,
My dove, my perfect one..."

Read and listen to the Word and write down the words or verses that inspire and encourage you.

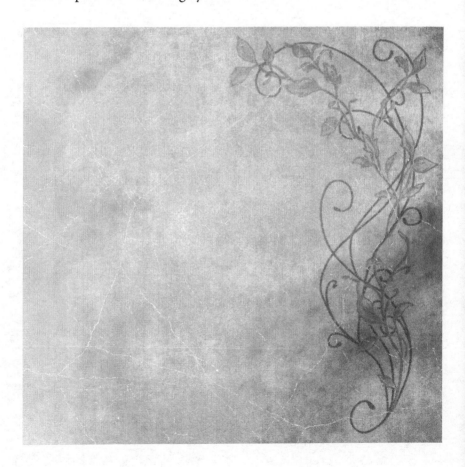

P – Where do you see a prayer in this chapter?

_____

_____

_____

R – Where do you see the relationship between you and Jesus? What verse do you see that in the most?

_____

_____

_____

Describe what prayer you see – feel – hear

_____

_____

_____

A – What attribute of God the Father do you see? What attribute of Jesus do you see?

_____

_____

_____

Y – What is God asking you to say 'yes' to in this chapter?

_____

_____

_____

Journal

Write out a portion or all of chapter 5 as a prayer below, writing each verse back to God in prayer.

Song of Solomon chapter 6

"Where has your beloved gone,
O fairest among women?
Where has your beloved turned aside,
That we may seek him with you?"

Read and listen to the Word and write down the words or verses that inspire and encourage you.

P – Where do you see a prayer in this chapter?

_____

_____

_____

R – Where do you see the relationship between you and Jesus? What verse do you see that in the most?

_____

_____

_____

Describe what prayer you see – feel – hear

_____

_____

_____

A – What attribute of God the Father do you see? What attribute of Jesus do you see?

_____

_____

_____

Y – What is God asking you to say 'yes' to in this chapter?

_____

_____

_____

Journal

Write out a portion or all of chapter 6 as a prayer below, writing each verse back to God in prayer.

Song of Solomon chapter 7

"I am my beloved's,
And his desire is toward me."

Read and listen to the Word and write down the words or verses that inspire and encourage you.

P – Where do you see a prayer in this chapter?

_____

_____

_____

R – Where do you see the relationship between you and Jesus? What verse do you see that in the most?

_____

_____

_____

Describe what prayer you see – feel – hear

_____

_____

_____

A – What attribute of God the Father do you see? What attribute of Jesus do you see?

_____

_____

_____

Y – What is God asking you to say 'yes' to in this chapter?

_____

_____

_____

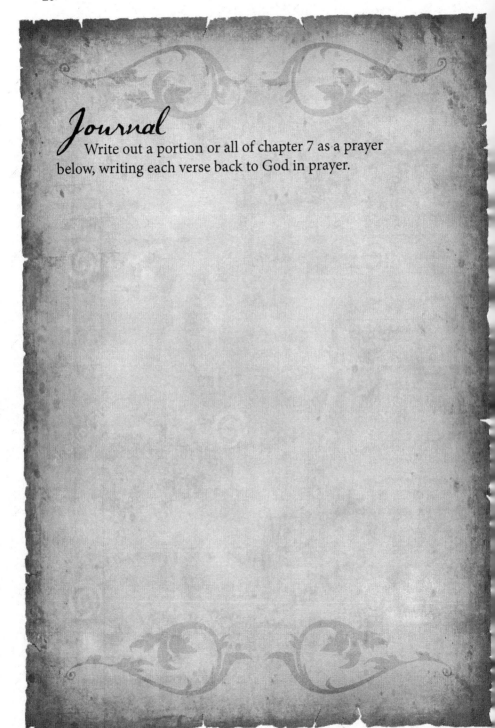

Journal

Write out a portion or all of chapter 7 as a prayer below, writing each verse back to God in prayer.

Song of Songs chapter 8

"Set me as a seal upon your heart,
As a seal upon your arm;
For love is as strong as death,
Jealousy as cruel as the grave;
Its flames are flames of fire,
A most vehement flame.
Many waters cannot quench love..."

Read and listen to the Word and write down the words or verses that inspire and encourage you.

P – Where do you see a prayer in this chapter?

_____

_____

_____

R – Where do you see the relationship between you and Jesus? What verse do you see that in the most?

_____

_____

_____

Describe what prayer you see – feel – hear

_____

_____

_____

A – What attribute of God the Father do you see? What attribute of Jesus do you see?

_____

_____

_____

Y – What is God asking you to say 'yes' to in this chapter?

_____

_____

_____

Journal

Write out a portion or all of chapter 8 as a prayer below, writing each verse back to God in prayer.

Congratulations!

You have just read, prayed and journaled through the entire Book of Song of Solomon!

I hope this journey has challenged and changed you in your prayer life and reading the Word daily.

I encourage you to go back and reflect on what you wrote each day. Look at your notes and relive what you experienced in that moment. It is interesting to go back over what I wrote and reflect on my heart, feelings and thoughts at that time, then compare all of that to when this journey began. God will show you how you changed through what you just read.

If you could narrow the entire book down to one moment, one thought, what would that be?

_____

I want to pray for you.

Father, In the name of Jesus, I pray that what my friend has learned in the journey through this precious book, will go deep into her heart.

I pray that as she reflects on her notes and thoughts, even more revelation of love will flow from You to them. I pray that what you have begun in her, you will bring to completion. I pray that everything you showed her and taught her will not depart, but will deepen within her heart.

Bless my friend as she continues in the pursuit of You through Your Word.

To connect with the author
or for seminar and retreat information

Kim Zimmerman
218 N. Duke Street
Lancaster, PA 17602

Info@citygatelancaster.com
www.facebook.com/Kim-Zimmerman

56190718R00024

Made in the USA
Lexington, KY
15 October 2016